123 SESAME STREET®

Rainy Day Crafts

First published by Parragon in 2009

Parragon
Queen Street House
4 Queen Street
Bath BA1 1HE, UK

ISBN 978-1-4075-7200-0

Printed in China

123 SESAME STREET®

Rainy Day Crafts

PaRragon

Bath · New York · Singapore · Hong Kong · Cologne · Delhi · Melbourne

Prepare your space

Cover your workspace with newspaper or a plastic or paper tablecloth. Make sure you and your children are wearing clothes (including shoes!) that you don't mind becoming spattered with food, paint, or glue. But relax! You'll never completely avoid mess; in fact, it's part of the fun!

Wash your hands

Wash your hands (and your child's hands) before starting a new project, and clean up as you go along. Clean hands make for clean crafts! Remember to wash your hands afterward, too, using soap and warm water to get off any of the remaining materials.

Follow steps carefully

Follow each step carefully, and in the sequence in which it appears. We've tested all the projects; we know they work, and we want them to work for you, too. Also, ask your children, if they are old enough, to read along with you as you work through the steps. For a younger child, you can direct her to look at the pictures on the page to try to guess what the next step is.

Measure precisely

If a project gives you measurements, use your ruler, T-square, measuring cups, or measuring spoons to make sure you measure as accurately as you can. Sometimes the success of the project may depend on it. Also, this is a great opportunity to teach measuring techniques to your child.

Be patient

You may need to wait while something bakes or leave paint, glue, or clay to dry, sometimes for a few hours or even overnight. Encourage your child to be patient as well; explain to her why she must wait, and, if possible, find ways to entertain her as you are waiting. For example you can show her how long you have to wait by pointing out the time on a clock.

Clean up

When you've finished your project, clean up any mess. Store all the materials together so that they are ready for the next time you want to craft. Ask your child to help.

TOY CARS

YOU WILL NEED

- Thin colored cardboard
- Pencil and ruler
- Scissors
- Masking tape
- Acrylic paint
- Paintbrushes
- 4 bottle or juice carton lids
- 2 drinking straws
- Modeling clay

①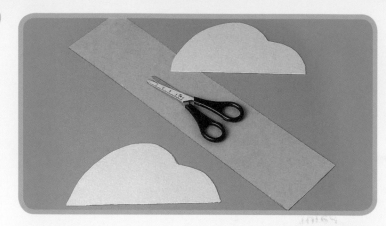

Draw two side views of a car on cardboard and a long thin rectangular strip to fit over the top.

②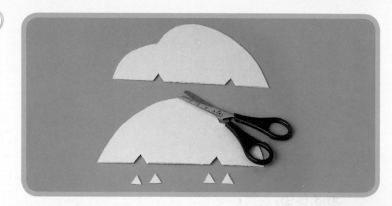

Cut the pieces out. Now cut out two small v-shapes in the same place on both shapes. This is where the wheels will be.

③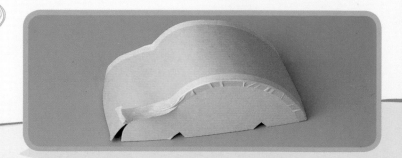

Use masking tape to fix the long rectangle to the top of the car sides, joining them together as shown. Then measure and cut a rectangle of cardboard to fit the bottom of the car.

4

KIDS

Paint the two side views and the rectangular piece that goes over the top.

5

KIDS

Stick a ball of modeling clay to the inside of each lid and push one end of the straw into the clay.

6

Push one straw all the way through the v-shape and attach the second wheel on the other side with modeling clay. Repeat with the second straw. Your car is now finished.

DID YOU KNOW? The first cars didn't have steering wheels. Drivers steered them with a lever.

Elmo loves cars! Vroom, vroom!

YOU WILL NEED

- Patterned fabric
- Scissors
- Uncooked lentils or other dried beans
- Needle and thread
- Spoon

1

Cut a rectangle of fabric and fold it in half, inside out. Sew seams along the side edges.

2

Turn the material right side out, ready to fill the bag.

3

KIDS

Use a spoon to half-fill the bag with the lentils or beans.

4

Neatly fold in the edges and sew them together firmly. Repeat to make more bags.

DID YOU KNOW? Juggling is fun and healthy. It's good for the heart, and helps you learn to concentrate.

Juggling not easy, so keep practicing!

BOWLING

YOU WILL NEED

- 6 or 10 large empty plastic drink bottles
- Acrylic paints
- Paintbrushes
- Sand

1 KIDS

Carefully wash out the bottles. When they are completely dry, screw on the lids tightly.

2 KIDS

Give each container a colorful base coat. You may need to paint each one with two or more layers of paint to cover it completely. Leave to dry.

3 KIDS

Now it's time to decorate your bowling pins. Paint on patterns and shapes in different colors. When all your bottles are painted, decorated, and dry, they are ready to use.

4
KIDS

Stand the bottles in a triangle shape, as shown in the picture. If you are using six bottles, place one at the front, two in the middle, and three in the back row. Use a small ball to play your bowling game. If they are too easy to knock over, fill them with a little sand to make them heavier.

DID YOU KNOW?
People have played bowling games since the days of ancient Egypt.

toys

YOU WILL NEED

- Dinner plate
- Thick blue cardboard
- Scissors
- Thin cardboard: blue, white
- Ruler and pencil
- Glue or adhesive tape
- Colored markers
- Colored adhesive tape (optional)
- Paper clips
- Garden stakes or other long sticks
- String

1

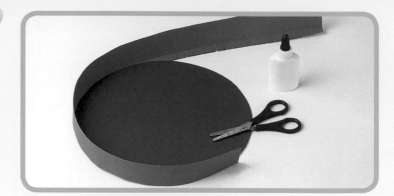

Draw around a plate on a piece of thick cardboard. Cut out the circle to make the base of the pond. Cut a long strip of thin cardboard to fit around the edge of the base and glue or tape it in place.

2 KIDS

Use colored tape or colored markers to decorate the sides.

3 KIDS

Draw ten fish and starfish on cardboard and cut them out. Decorate them with colored markers.

4

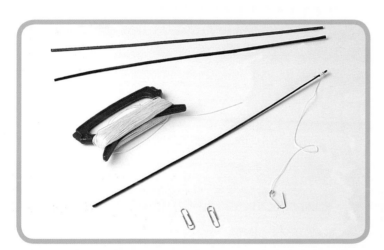

To add the loops to your cardboard fish, fold up the middle section of the paper clips and tape them to the back.

5

The fishing rods are made from garden stakes. Tie a paper clip to the end of a piece of string, then tape the string to the end of a garden stake. Shape the paper clip into a hook. Now you can go fishing!

Make lots of different sea creatures, such as fish, starfish, an octopus, or a crab.

AQUARIUM.

YOU WILL NEED

- Large shoe box and lid
- Scissors
- Acrylic paints and paintbrush
- Sheet of plastic wrap (blue if available)
- White glue
- Advesive tape
- Green tissue paper
- Pebbles
- Thin cardboard and paper
- Colored markers
- Glitter
- Gold thread
- Self-adhesive stars (optional)

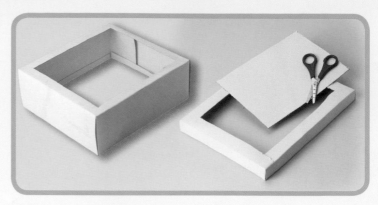

Cut a rectangle out of the box lid and the base of the box.

Paint the box and lid blue, inside and out.

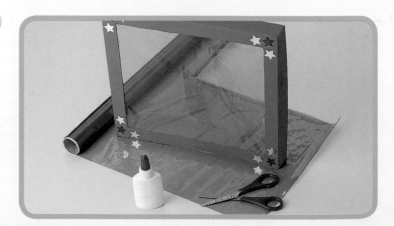

Glue a sheet of plastic wrap over the cut-out spaces.

4

KIDS

Cut tissue paper strips for the weeds. Tape them to the aquarium roof so they dangle down. Lay pebbles on the bottom.

5

KIDS

Draw fish on the thin cardboard and decorate them with paint and glitter.

6

Attach them to the roof with gold thread, then glue the lid on. Decorate with stars if you wish.

DID YOU KNOW?
Public aquariums can be enormous, with tanks the size of a football field!

YOU WILL NEED

- Wooden spoon
- Rolling pin
- Bowl
- Cookie cutters
- Baking sheet
- 1 ¼ cups plain flour
- 1 stick margarine or butter
- ⅓ cup sugar
- 1 teaspoon baking powder
- 1 egg
- Frosting, silver balls and sprinkles (optional)

- For plain cookies add:
  1 teaspoon vanilla extract
- For chocolate cookies add:
  3 tablespoons cocoa powder

1

Use a wooden spoon to mix the flour, margarine (or butter), vanilla extract (or cocoa powder), sugar, and baking powder, until it looks like breadcrumbs.

2

Add the egg and mix together until it forms a smooth dough.

3 KIDS

Sprinkle a little flour onto the work surface and roll out the dough with a rolling pin. Do not press too hard. Use your cutters to cut out a selection of shapes.

4

Place the cookies on a greased baking tray. Bake for 15 minutes at 350°F.

5 KIDS

Let cool and decorate with frosting, silver balls, and sprinkles.

DID YOU KNOW? In Great Britain, cookies are called "biscuits."

Homemade cookies make great gifts – if me don't eat them first!

YOU WILL NEED

- Two shoe boxes of same size
- Scissors
- Tape and glue
- Large paper clips
- Paint and paintbrushes
- Paper and cardboard
- Small boxes
- Colored markers

①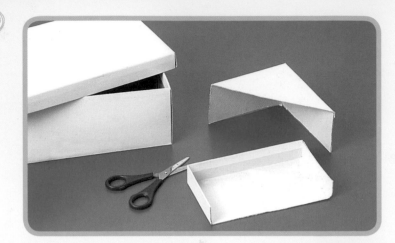

Use one of the shoe boxes to make the house. Cut a corner off the other box to make the roof.

②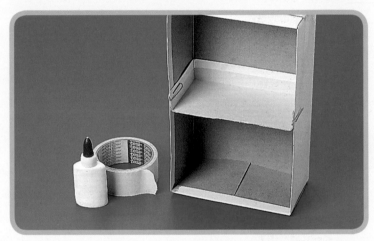

Cut one box lid so that it fits inside the house as the upstairs floor. Use glue and tape to stick the floor section into place. Hold the floor in position with the large paper clips while the glue is setting.

3
KIDS

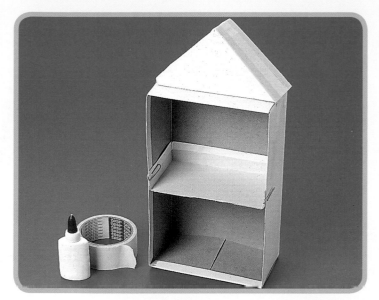

Use tape to attach the roof piece to the top of the house, as shown. Make sure you leave enough room at the front for the lid to fit.

4
KIDS

Make the front of the house from the other shoe box lid. Cut out squares for the windows, then paint the roof and walls. Decorate the inside of your dollhouse. Use colored paper for wallpaper, fabric to make rugs, and small boxes for furniture.

DID YOU KNOW?
Queen Mary of England's dollhouse had working lights and elevators, and even flushing toilets!

CLOTH DOLL

YOU WILL NEED

- Fabric in a flesh color
- Colored marker
- Scissors
- Needle and thread
- Polyester stuffing
- Patterned fabric
- Fabric paint
- Paintbrush
- Wool
- Cardboard 3 x 3 inches
- Ribbon

①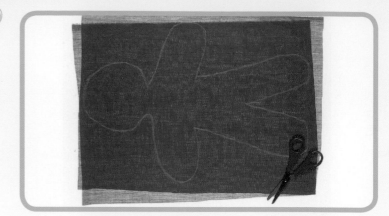

Draw a doll shape onto a double layer of fabric.

②

Sew around the drawn line, leaving an extra half inch gap to turn the fabric out. Fill it with stuffing, then cut out the doll.

③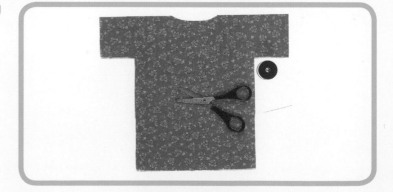

Draw a dress on the patterned fabric. Cut out and sew the edges together, inside out, leaving the neck, bottom, and the sleeve ends open.

(4)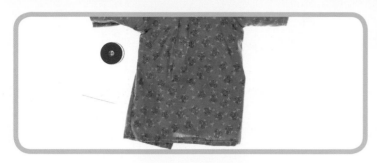

Turn the dress the right way out and sew a hem along the bottom of the fabric.

(5)

Paint the doll's face, then make her hair by winding the wool around a piece of cardboard and sewing a line down the middle for a "part." Attach the hair with glue.

 6
KIDS

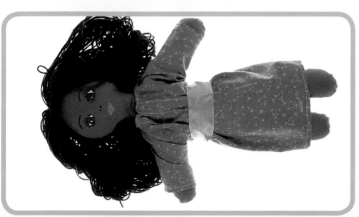

Dress your doll and tie a ribbon belt around her waist.

DID YOU KNOW?
Before the word doll was invented, people called dolls "puppets" or "babies."

You can also use the fabric shape in step 1 to make a gingerbread man shape. Then you can decorate him!

YOU WILL NEED

- Bowl
- Tablespoon
- Rolling pin
- Small plate
- Knife
- Baking sheet
- Fork
- Pastry brush

Pastry:
- 1½ cups plain flour
- ¾ cup margarine or butter
- 1 teaspoon water

Filling:
- 1 cup cooked, diced potato
- 1 medium onion, chopped
- 1 cup cheese, grated
- 1 egg, beaten
- Salt and pepper (to taste)

1

Place the flour and margarine (or butter) in a bowl, and use your fingers to mix it until it looks like breadcrumbs. Add a tablespoon of water and mix well, to make a ball.

2

Roll out the pastry to a thickness of a quarter of an inch. Use a plate to mark out circles. Cut them out with a knife.

KIDS

3

Measure the filling ingredients and add them to a bowl. Mix them well, adding salt and pepper to taste.

Place the pastry circles on a greased baking sheet. Put a spoonful of filling in the middle of each. Brush a little beaten egg on the edges of the pastry.

5

Fold over the pastry to cover the filling. Use the fork to press down and seal the edges. Brush beaten egg over each finished empanada and bake for 25 minutes at 350°F, until golden brown.

DID YOU KNOW?
An empanada is a stuffed bread or pastry. It comes from Spain.

Use any bits of leftover pastry to make jam tarts.

YOU WILL NEED

- Thin cardboard
- Paper
- Pencil
- Wax crayons or pencils
- Sheets of white paper
- Scissors

1

KIDS

Draw a teddy bear onto cardboard. Give it a face and color it in.

2

Cut out the bear with scissors. Make as many bears as you want in this way.

Lay the cut-out teddy bears onto the white paper and draw an outfit around each one. Draw tabs on each outfit as shown, color in the outfits, then cut them out.

4

KIDS

Dress your teddy bears in their new outfits, by folding back the tabs behind the bears.

DID YOU KNOW?
The teddy bear was named after American President Theodore Roosevelt.

YOU WILL NEED

- Big box
- White glue and brush
- Old newspaper
- Acrylic paints and paintbrush
- 1 sheet white paper and pencil
- Scissors
- Sponge
- Small plate
- Adhesive tape

1 KIDS

Glue two layers of newspaper inside and outside the box, covering it completely. Do this in stages, allowing the box to dry in a warm, airy place between each layer.

2 KIDS

When the layers are completely dry, paint the box. You may need two or three coats of paint to cover the newspaper completely. Remember to let the paint dry between coats.

③

Draw a simple stencil design onto the center of a sheet of paper and cut it out. You may want to make a few stencils with different shapes.

④

Loosely tape the stencil to the side of the box. Dip the sponge in a little paint and pat it on the plate to get rid of any extra, then dab it over the stencil. Practice on scrap paper before decorating your toy box.

DID YOU KNOW? Keeping your toys in a toy box is a great way to keep them from getting broken!

YOU WILL NEED

- Shoe box lid
- Acrylic paints and paintbrushes
- Thin strip of craft wood (long enough to go around the cardboard rectangle)
- Pencil
- Ruler
- Scissors
- Glue
- Small box
- 16 buttons in 2 different colors (8 of each color)

KIDS

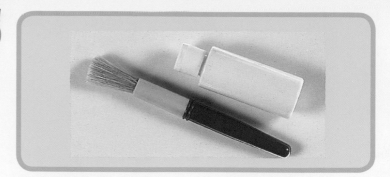

Paint the shoe box lid white to make the base of the game board, then paint the edging strip of craft wood in a darker color. Leave to dry.

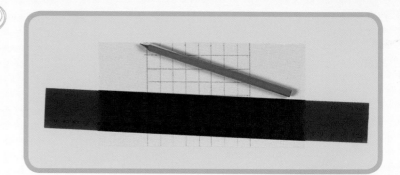

Use a ruler to measure and mark out the game board with eight rows of eight squares. Leave space at each end of the board for your pieces.

When you've drawn the squares, paint every other square a darker color, as shown.

4

Cut the wooden edging strip into four pieces and glue in place to form the board edges. Decorate the board at each end, if you wish.

5

KIDS

Paint a small box in the darker color and decorate it to match your game board. Use this box to store your checkers. Each player will need eight checkers. Make sure each set of checkers is a different color.

DID YOU KNOW?
An eight square board can be used to play lots of games, including chess.

Why not make your own checkers from painted pebbles if you like?

YOU WILL NEED

- Oven-bake clay in a variety of colors
- Modeling tool
- Baking sheet
- Aluminum foil
- Magnets
- Strong white glue

1 KIDS

Knead the clay in your hand until it is soft enough to shape.

2 KIDS

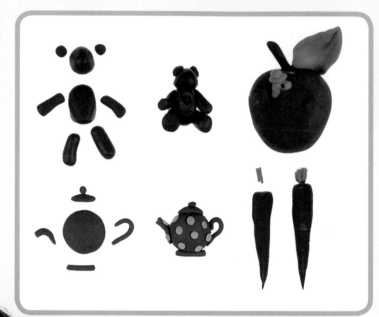

Experiment with the clay to make different items to decorate your fridge magnets. You could try making animals, faces, a teapot, fruits, or vegetables. You could even make a teddy bear from brown clay.

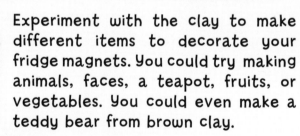

③

Press a magnet into the back of each clay item, then remove it before baking. Bake your objects in the oven, on a foil-covered baking sheet, following the manufacturer's instructions. Make sure you ask a grown-up for help. Once cool, glue the magnet in place.

DID YOU KNOW? Magnets stick to anything made of, or containing, a metal called iron.

Elmo is going to make the letters of his name: ELMO.

INDEX